Beneath It All

A Collection of Poems
by K Wendt

LONE MESA PUBLISHING

www.lonemesapublishing.com

Beneath It All
ISBN: 978-0692634066
Copyright © 2016 K Wendt

Contact the author at k@ladybugwritings.com.

Contents

Let Us Ride

Give me a good horse
And a bad western any day
Let us ride
To the horizon line
Where the sun and moon dance for the twilight
And we'll tell our secrets to the wind
As it passes by
Let us ride
Into the night
Holding each other tight
Dance under the stars
That don't care who we are
Take a deep look into my eyes
See you're my desire for life
Let us ride
Sleep on the ground
Warmed by the love we have found
Dream of growing old
Never letting go
Keep traveling on
Cherishing our time alone
Let us ride

Blue Bonnets

In Texas every Spring,
Bloom flowers that make the countryside sing.
Never does one stand alone;
You'll find yourself swimming as you roam
Through fields of a brilliant blue,
Laughing and giggling such as children do.
And though they last just one season a year,
The memory of witnessing God's beauty
Is something you'll forever hold dear.

Dad

Daddy, Papa, Father,
Whatever his name,
He has the heart of his daughter;
No other can fill his frame.
He pretends to be hard and stern;
Occasions may warrant this,
But it's happiness for his children he yearns.
Inside, he's really a mushy mess.
A man of few words, yes indeed,
But listen when he speaks.
He'll support even the craziest of deeds;
The love for his family is the only thing that makes him
    weak.
He listens intently,
Respects who we are.
He loves unconditionally,
And is never far.
He encourages the chasing of dreams
And tries to protect us from hurt.
I had a few glimpses of cheeks stained with tear streams;
He's a true man with a soft heart.
I love you, Dad.
Thank you for loving me,
Encouraging me to explore paths I never have,
And helping me teach my children the meaning of family.

The Family Tree

As God created Adam from the dust of the ground,
So He planted a seed that would firmly abound.
With love, God watered that seed,
And it grew sprouting a leaf.
As years went by, that seed became a beautiful tree,
It's limbs and leaves reaching upward in glee.
God gave that tree the strength to withstand harsh seasons
     and mighty winds.
Old leaves fall away and birth of new ones begin.
Though the tree seems to stretch out forever from limb to
     limb,
Every part of it moves as one within.
This mighty tree that God loves so dear
Stands as an example for families to share.
Like the tree, the family started young and vulnerable.
With God's love, the family grew in strength and began
     loving unconditional.
Life experiences attempted to pull the family down
But their deep-rooted love kept them on solid ground.
Each year, new members are added as old ones fade away;
Life choices create separate paths;
But, as does the tree, the family remains as one and shares
     their love just as God has.

Pray

Pray
Pray for those who stumble
And those who fall
Pray for those who are humble
And hear the call
Pray for the quick mumbles
And the shouts off the walls
Pray as things crumble
And God needs us most of all
Pray

Key

Excuse me, sir,

I've lost something important to me.

Have you by chance seen it?

It's a most precious object:

A key special-made

To fit a lock in an unique way—

A lock fitted for a great treasure chest.

Without these treasures, I cannot fully exist.

The absence of these treasures stops my heartbeat;

They are necessary to move my feet.

They cannot remain locked away,

For who I am will fade.

Without them, life is rough, and it's hard to breathe.

So, I ask again, have you seen my key?

It is my joy, my peace, my serenity.

It connects me to my Lord and Master,

Helps me be a little wiser.

Oh, sir, are you sure you haven't seen my key?

How can that be?

I left it here not that long ago.

It was when my Master commanded I obey, and I said no.

It's been miserable since.

Without my key, I cannot repent.

Oh, sir, please help me find it.

I can hear my blood starting to drip,

My soul is leaving me.

My Master is grieving.

Sir, find my key!

Set me free!
Without it, I am only skin and bones;
My heart no longer has a home;
And the spirit flies away,
Because I was not able to obey.

Angel

The angel was there
I could see him
I felt his stare
He stood opposite the demon
He had come to rescue me
By my Savior's orders
He was trying to set me free
His eyes were like embers
As they reflected the demon before him
His right side crimson
From the sword of the demon
His strength had been weakened
Yet the angel towered above us
Demanding obedience
The demon only laughed and cussed
Standing in defiance
The demon raised his sword
The angel began to pray
As I cowered to the floor
A fight between good and evil was displayed
Sounds of rage, and anguish declared war
Then…nothing…complete silence
I removed my hands from my face
And shuttered as I found the demon's deadly compliance
I looked to the angel as my heart began to race
He reached down and scooped me up
He told me my Savior missed me
That His is an unending love

Only with my Savior am I truly free
The angel delivered me back to the arms of my Savior
There is no other place I would rather be

Church

This room is stuffy
There is no way to breath
The air is hazy
I need to break free
They hold me there
In that room
I feel the heat of their stare
I sense impending doom
I beg, I plead
I pull away
They want me to bleed
They see me as a stray
They believe their ritual
Is intoxicating
Instead of spiritual
It's suffocating
There's an alter call
They rush past
I run before I fall
The spell, they could not cast
I run across the river
Up to the mountain top
It's there I'm delivered
I water the ground with my tear drops
I laugh and cry
As I listen
To my Creator's sighs
The sun glistens

On the blades of grass
The wind whispers
The judgement passed
Forgiveness for this sinner
Flower scents
Kiss tear-stained cheeks
This is my repent
This is the church I seek

Demons and Desires

Tell me, my Lord, what do I see?

Is it real? Is it my destiny?

No, please, Lord, don't set me free!

I need you, Father, to stay with me.

I don't want to go alone;

I am not ready to leave from home.

Why are You pushing me from the only love I have known?

No, Father, don't set me free!

Please, please, I cannot see!

Hug me and let me cling to You for all my life;

I can't handle any strife.

I need You, my Lord, I need You!

I don't want to be a part of this cruel, heartless world.

It's ugly and deceitful;

I am not wise enough to know demon from desire.

Please, Lord, I don't have what the world requires.

I am not ready to be released;

I want to stay in Your peace.

Please, Lord, don't push me away!

I want to stay! I want to stay!

My Father! My Gracious Lord!

Only You I want to adore.

I am sorry, Lord, for being so bad, so ugly,

But, Father, don't leave me,

Don't leave me to be devoured,

For surely the world will crave me in my first hour.

I am not strong enough;

And they play rough.

Father, there is no difference between demons and desires!
I will not survive their hypnotic fire.
They don't call You sire.
They don't love You like I wish to.
They seek not the warmth of You like I do.
They don't call Your name
To wake them from their nightmare.
Why, my Lord, why are You sending me there!?
I am pleading with You, Lord, let me stay.
I promise, I promise to obey.
I did not mean to hurt You, Lord, and make You cry;
I knew my heart would betray my lies!
Forgive, my Father, please!
I fall to my knees
And beg Your mercy.
It was not You I meant to deceive.
Forgive me, my Lord, I cannot replace
The hurt I caused when I was left on my own;
Demons and desires intertwine, I should have known.
Oh, my Lord, my Lord! I am so sorry
I was only thinking of me.
Take me back, Lord, don't push me away!
I need to stay;
I am no good on my own.
The capability You entrusted with me has not shown.
My Father, they had me right away,
Convinced me my desires were okay.
Those awful demons and how they betray!
Forgive me, my Lord, hold on to me,

Show me again the love I need.
Comfort me, Father, and heal my wounds.
Their grip on me is loosening, it will be gone soon!
Father, Father, hold me close,
Tell me You love me in overdose.
Wrap Your arms around me and rock me like a child
I have not felt Your comfort for a while.
Love me, Lord, forgive me,
Take me, Lord, and consume me,
Don't let me be torn apart again.
I fear the next time, I will not mend!
Father, my Father, take care of me,
Living without you is not my ability!

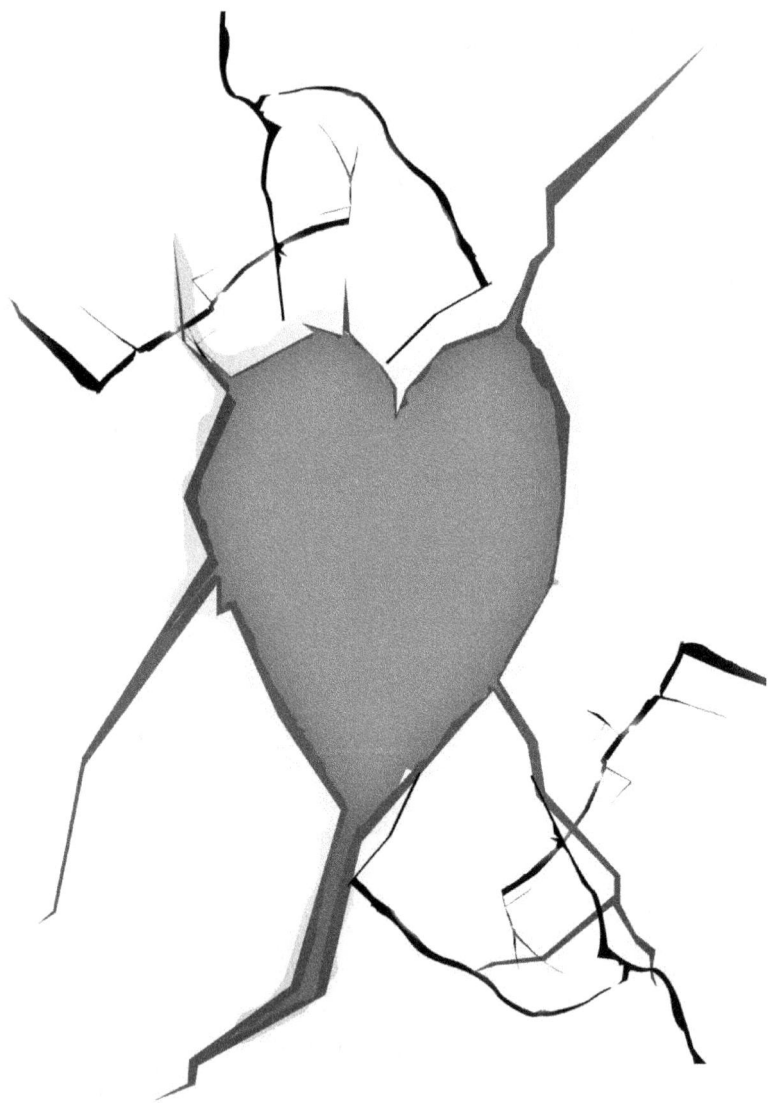

Broken Pieces

Love's laughter mixes with the creek's giggle
As bound-up emotion slowly unravels.
They were destined
To be one again.
Together they mend
The broken pieces their hearts had been shattered in.
Little by little, they sew their love back together,
Dreaming of forever,
Hearts and hands interlocked.
Soft kisses make up time that was lost,
Gentle, caressing touches.
A love once forbidden rushes to hold on
As they mend their broken pieces.
The creek's current releases
All the tears and sorrow
That had replaced love's hollow.
They show their love unashamed
Joyful this day came,
And they become one again,
Their hearts stronger with mended broken pieces.

His Love

Time stands still
The ocean grabs her with its salty hands
She takes in the air
Letting the ocean drown her there
Down and under with the current
Swept by emotions
To the dark of the ocean
No light
Darkness encompasses
Falling, she releases all
And lets the ocean set her free
Yet from the deep within the ocean's blue
A sound so familiar
A word echoes from above
Her heart awakens
The grip of the ocean releases
Gently, she rises
The waves return her to shore
As she lays upon the sand
The word sounds again
The voice of one calls to her
Beckoning home his love

Found Love

Life is a journey unmapped
Full of twisted turns and mishaps.
As we try to unwind some of the tangles we create,
We sometimes find things some would call fate.

Some are fortunate along their paths
To find a love that begs to last.
No one knows when their lives will be blessed
To feel such overwhelming happiness.

It is a love that wraps you up in warmth
Does all it can to protect you from harm.
This is a love that never dies;
It is what keeps your heart alive.

If unfortunate, you slipped away
And your true love could not stay,
Remember the times you spent;
Cherish what it meant.

Age of Love

Love has transcended lifetimes;
It exists without reason or rhyme;
It cannot be possessed;
It does not live or die.
Love is something that overcomes
When not expected.
Love knows better
What is good and what isn't.
It has no limitations
Or discriminations.
Love is so beautiful when freely given.
Love wants to be needed,
Beautifully treated;
Love wants silly giggles;
Love needs to wrap up in warmth;
Love wants to hear the heartbeat.
Such a blessing,
Yet a curse;
The possessors are unworthy
Of such timeless beauty.

Walk With Me

Would you like to walk with me among the roses?
Maybe run barefoot in the sand?
Drink in the air of the ocean?
Discover a peace within this land?
Escape to our Neverland,
Trace life's path,
Stop time's hand?
Let us tease and laugh,
Silly things done.
Embrace all we have,
And victories won.
Walk with me,
Allow me to show you my love.
Feel free
To tell me you love me, too.

Beneath it All

Atop a hill looking down,
Surrounded by a quilt of flowers all around,
The creek giggles on the rocks below.
Do you feel safe as a sweet wind blows?
Are you wrapped up in the flowers' warmth?
Secured by the never-ending glass in the creek,
Breathing in deeply perfumed air.
Or are you afraid of the ground beneath the flowers?
That beneath their beauty may lay a snake waiting to strike.
If you take that drink, will you drown in the bottomless
    supply?
Is the air really that sweet, or is it suffocating you inside?
Do you run from your fears or secure yourself in the apparent
    peace?
Do you wrap yourself up
And pretend there is nothing there at all?
Nothing to scare you,
Nothing to deceive you,
Nothing but grayness you couldn't see before.
Was it worth it?
Or do you find yourself wanting that sweet-smelling quilt
    that kept you warm?
That cool glass of water that quenched your every thirst?

Woman

What makes a woman?

Does she have to be as fragile as china?

Or soft as cotton?

Her beauty captured on dolls;

Is she not allowed to have flaws?

Why can't a woman speak out and say

"You are wrong, sir! For portraying me this way!"

Why can't a woman be as strong as a man?

Were they not both created by God's hand?

A woman's beauty lies not within her face;

She is more than perfume and lace.

Her heart beats strong with her every desire.

Her intelligent mind is worth being inquired.

She feels everything that happens in her life;

The lines tracing her smile are mixtures of love and strife.

With her strength, she brings forth a child,

And her temper is less than mild,

For she is passionate and loves with her whole self;

She cannot be replaced with someone else.

A woman is the strength a man lacks;

She loves him completely and never looks back.

A woman gives herself entirely to those she loves;

No creature can do the things she's capable of.

The Music Created

She waited impatiently
To hear a sound connected to old memories
The sound would catch her
Take hold of her
She'd spin with eyes shut
Letting the sound wrap her up
Through the rhythm
The musician created
She would disappear
Let it take her miles away from here
So, impatiently she waited
For the music to be created

Prayer of a Broken Woman

She's down on her knees
Beaten, battered, and bruised
Losing life in a battle against disease
Crying toward heaven
She says
Lord, I strayed so long ago
Can I still come home?
It is the prayer of a broken woman
Finding her way home
It takes crying toward heaven
To realize she can't do it alone
She kisses him goodbye
As he leaves for his nine-to-five
There's got to be a better way
To survive this day and age
Drowning in this pile of debt
How much deeper could this hole get?
Crying toward heaven
She says
Lord, I strayed so long ago
Can I still come home?
It is the prayer of a broken woman
Finding her way home
It takes crying toward heaven
To realize she can't do it alone
It's just her and Abby now
Abby thanks God for having the bestest mom
She giggles at the innocence of her child

Says "Good night. I love you," and leaves the nightlight on
She goes to bed with misty eyes
How in the world is she going to give Abby everything she
    needs?
Crying toward heaven
She says
Lord, I strayed so long ago
Can I still come home?
It is the prayer of a broken woman

Life

Life-struggle
Struggle-life
No longer able to juggle
No longer able to handle strife
Life's mystery
Has been opened wide
The fairy tale is history
There is no longer a place to hide
Life-struggle
Struggle-life

Give

I always seem to give
Both in and to
Sought for comfort
Sought for truth
I give, give, give
Thinking I'd receive
But the only thing here
Is hurt and fear
I question my creation
If God only made me to give
Then why am I so anxious to receive
Giving drains
And I cannot function
Surely I deserve reciprocation
Why would I be created to live in misery
Only to be others sanctity
If evil is my seed
Why then create in me a need
Breath in, breath out
Breath in, breath out
It's time to give again
And I have to do without

I Am

Stuck in the middle
Two worlds at my side
One to be followed
The other pushed aside
Yet, I cannot fully follow the one
Without leaving pieces of me
My life run
By others thinking
I do not know who I am
But I cannot exist solely in one world
Let me stay as I am
A mixed-up girl
Not yet clearly defined
I desire to follow
But the thinking must be mine
Or my mind becomes hollow
Let me have as I desire
Let me be who I am
Light the two worlds on fire
Let me fill the flames
Consume me
Envelope me
Create me
Mold into me
Let me become who I am

Lonely Hell

She's tired of the loneliness.
How'd she get herself in this?
Lives move around her;
Loneliness drags her deeper
Into an abyss.
There, awaiting, a deadly kiss,
She fights to free herself,
Afraid of a lonely hell.
She screams and no one hears.
Instead, she awakens her fears.
Oh God, don't let her be alone.
Surely, love exists in one she's known.

Forgotten

Forgotten.
Please don't let me be forgotten
I'm so lost today
Don't let yesterday fade away
I pray I'm not a stain
Don't refrain
From letting memories of me
Flood your sleep

Forgotten
Don't let me be forgotten
Every day is a day further away
If only time could stay
Grounded to the memory
So you could remember me
Don't let me be forgotten

Forgotten

Who Am I

Who am I?
There is part of me
That wants to be able to live more free;
Another part feels locked up with a lost key.
Is it a shame
That I enjoy games.
Should I have myself hold tighter reigns?
Do I put certain people to shame?
My desire was not
Meant for the attention it got.
They are bothering quite a lot,
But it seems no answer can be sought.
Can I not live and laugh
Without fearing the wrath?
Do I regret my should-not-haves?
I wasn't trying to go down any certain paths;
I just want to have fun.
Yet, I always feel that is something I shouldn't have done.
What's wrong with feeling young?
      And wanting to freely run?
I admit my mistake;
I was not trying to get anyone raked.
I decided to be a part of the joking;
I didn't mean for anyone to become provoking.
So, I will silence myself and go on my way;
I knew it was too good to stay.
I am evil and obviously do not behave;
I am sorry I got in the way.

About the Author

K Wendt has been writing since she was in high school, starting with lyrics and poems. In the Spring of 2013, the idea for *Duney*, her first children's book, came to her and she said she had to see it through, especially when her son, Monte, agreed to illustrate it.

Since then, Wendt has been inspired chase her desire to write, and will finish her first adult novel soon. In the meantime, she has published her fourth children's book, *Billy*, in addition to this collection of poems.

Find more of K's work and her blog on her Website at *www.ladybugwritings.com.*

www.ingramcontent.com/pod-product-compliance
Lightning Source LLC
Chambersburg PA
CBHW060643030426
42337CB00018B/3421